William Higgins

An Essay on the Theory and Practice of Bleaching

William Higgins

An Essay on the Theory and Practice of Bleaching

ISBN/EAN: 9783742816139

Manufactured in Europe, USA, Canada, Australia, Japa

Cover: Foto ©Thomas Meinert / pixelio.de

Manufactured and distributed by brebook publishing software
(www.brebook.com)

William Higgins

An Essay on the Theory and Practice of Bleaching

AN

ESSAY

ON THE

THEORY AND PRACTICE

OF

BLEACHING,

WHEREIN

THE SULPHURET OF LIME IS RECOMMENDED

AS A

SUBSTITUTE FOR POT-ASH.

———— ⚙ ————

BY *WILLIAM HIGGINS*, M. R. I. A.

PROFESSOR OF CHEMISTRY AND MINERALOGY AT THE
REPOSITORY OF THE DUBLIN SOCIETY.

———— ⚙ ————

London:

PRINTED FOR THE AUTHOR;

AND SOLD BY

VERNOR AND HOOD, NO. 31, POULTRY.

1799.

PRICE TWO SHILLINGS.

TO THE

RIGHT HONORABLE AND HONORABLE

THE

LINEN BOARD,

THE FOLLOWING

E S S A Y

IS INSCRIBED BY

THEIR MUCH OBLIGED,

AND VERY HUMBLE SERVANT,

THE AUTHOR.

CONTENTS.

PREFACE.

SOON after I fent in a report on the *fulphuret of lime* to the Linen Board, they requefted to have fome experiments made upon it in their prefence, at the Elaboratory of the Dublin Society in Hawkins's-ftreet; which led to a lecture upon the general principles of bleaching, illuftrated with fuitable experiments.

At that time, I had no idea of publifhing any thing upon the fubject; but finding that it was the wifh of the Rt. Hon. John Fofter, Speaker of the

House

Houſe of Commons, and of the Rt.
Hon. Iſaac Corry, who were preſent,
to have it printed for the uſe of the
bleachers, I readily aſſented, feeling
great ſatisfaction in having it in my
power to comply with the wiſhes of
heſe gentlemen, but particularly with
the wiſh of the man * who has ſo materially contributed to the preſent
proſperous ſtate of the Linen Manufacture of this kingdom, and who ſo
diſintereſtedly makes it his ſtudy to
forward every other manufacture and
inſtitution likely to be productive of
national good.

I alſo undertook the taſk with ſome
degree of alacrity, when I conſidered
that any treatiſe likely to throw light
upon the principles of this art, muſt not
only be acceptable, but ultimately of
infinite

* The Rt. Hon. the Speaker.

infinite fervice to the bleacher, whofe procefs is truly chemical in all its ftages.

When I firft fat down to write, I intended to confine myfelf to the mere bleaching of the cloth by means of the oxygenated muriate of lime, and the *fulphuret of lime*; but I afterwards conceived, that it would be much better to give a full narrative and theory of the whole procefs in the old and new method, and alfo, to commence with the green *flax* fo as to begin at the right end of the chain, and to avoid chafms, to take it up link after link, according to the pofition or arrangement which the finger of nature feemed to point out to me.

In fo fhort an effay confined to the one object, this could be no difficult tafk; however, I will obferve, that in

b all

all fcientific works, much depends upon good arrangement, for without it, there can be no perfpicuity; and as chemiftry embraces fuch a vaft field, indeed I may fay, all the materials of this globe, and moft of the phœnomena which come within our reach, in no one branch of fcience is arrangement more neceffary, or more difficult to be ac- complifhed.

As the following effay was written for the ufe of the bleachers only, and as the majority of them are not well acquainted with the theory of chemif- try, I have endeavoured to write it in as fimple and familiar a ftile as the nature of the fubject would admit: I have overlooked minutiæ altogether unne- cefsary to the bleacher, which, I fhould hope, the man of fcience will excufe.

The

The few technical terms, which I was obliged to ufe, are explained at the bottom of the page, which I confidered more convenient to the reader than to have them fet apart by themfelves.

I now beg leave to fay a few words to my philofophical friends. Nine years have elapfed fince I addreffed them laft; at that time, when I publifhed my *Comparative View*, the controverfy ran very high between the *Phlogiftians* and the *Antiphlogiftians*. For a confiderable time have I ftood alone in England, where I then refided, being the firft who adopted the antiphlogiftic doctrine, and the only man who had exprefsly written in favour of it in the Englifh language.

During this interval, nothing worthy of notice has appeared for or againft either

either doctrine, and now, the antiphlogiftic theory is received by all the philofophers of Europe, at leaft, by thofe
who deferve the name of philofophers.

I have feen, with pleafure, that, fince
the controverfy was laid afide, and the
true theory of chemiftry adopted and
fixed upon a firm bafis, moft chemical
philofophers have applied their knowledge and talents to the improvement of
the arts and manufactures, which is the
ultimate and grand object of the fcience.

I have feen alfo, with great aftonifh-
ment, that fome experiments which I
made and publifhed, were a confiderable time afterwards adduced as *new*
difcoveries on the continent.

Firft, *Monfieur Fourcroy* publifhed in
the year 1791*, as a new difcovery,
the

---

* *See Medecin eclairé par les fciences phifiques*
Tom. 2*d. pag.* 321. *No.* X 1.

the prefence of bile in the blood; or rather, the converfion of fome of the principles of the blood into a fubftance refembling bile: This I had done fome years before him by the mediation of the nitrous acid. For the truth of what I affert, fee pages 162 and 163 of my *Comparative View*, publifhed in the year 1789.

Secondly, *Monfieur Vanquilin* has publifhed as his difcovery, in the *Journal des Mines* " *a new method of determining the quantity of carbon contained in fteel.*" See the extract from it in the *Annales de Chemie* for the year 1797. This *new* method is by means of the volatile fulphureous acid, and for the difcovery I will refer to my *Comparative View*, pages 49, 50 and 51, where the juftice of my claim will evidently appear.

I by

I by no means impeach the above philofophers with plagiarifm; I have too much refpect for the high character they have acquired in the fcientific world to fufpect them of fuch conduct, but that it has been, at leaft, an over-fight, muft be allowed.

The chemical properties of the ful-phureous acid were very little known, if at all, when I publifhed my experiments upon the fubject. It firft drew my attention with a view folely of inveftigating the truth of the *antiphlogiftic theory*, and it furnifhed me with *incontrovertible* arguments in favor of that doctrine. Amongft its various properties, that of diffolving iron without the *production* of hydrogen gas, at the fame time that the *whole* of the carbon and fulphur contained in the iron were left behind,

behind, impreffed me moft, by pointing out the importance of it as a *menftruum* for the analyfis of iron or fteel in an eafy, fimple, and certain way.

The celebrated Bergman laboured hard to analyfe the different kinds of iron and fteel, and made the moft of the menftrua which the chemiftry of his days afforded: He afcertained only the prefence of thofe fubftances contained in iron ; nor was it poffible to find out their proportion by any means hitherto difcovered, until the happy application of the fulphureous acid in that way.

Sulphuric acid confifts of one part of fulphur, and two of oxygen chemically united. When iron is introduced into this acid diluted with four or five times its bulk of water, it is diffolved, and

hydrogen

hydrogen gas is copiously produced, which is now allowed to come from the water. The sulphureous acid contains but equal parts of oxygen and sulphur*, that is, one half the quantity of oxygen which the sulphuric acid contains, and yet it dissolves the iron without the decomposition of water. These two facts contrasted, opened to my view quite a new theory, which I have already submitted to the opinion of the scientific world, and as an explanation of it would be too long for my present limits, I will refer to my *Comparative View*, from page 36 to page 61.

Let us now consider how far the French method of accounting for the decompofition of water may be reconciled to the above facts.

The

* This I have shewn by experiment. See my *Comparative View*, pages 80 and 81.

The French philofophers fuppofe, from the attraction of fulpuric acid for an *oxyd* of iron, that this metal decompofes the water in order to oxygenate itfelf, at the inftant of its union to the acid, and thus liberates its hydrogen: This, they tell us, takes place, by virtue of a predifpofing affinity: that fuch an affinity exifts, I know by experience; but it does not prevail here*, for the fulphureous acid, as containing lefs oxygen, and confequently having ftronger affinity to metallic oxyds, fhould, upon the above principle, be a more powerful agent in decom-

---

* The brilliant experiment of Mr. Tennant, of Cambridge, by which he decompofed carbonic acid gas, by paffing the vapour of phofphorus through heated carbonate of lime, the oxygenation of iron pyrites, and the formation of nitrous acid, from the union of the *azote* and *oxygen* of the atmofphere by calcareous matter, are all ftriking inftances of this kind of affinity.

c

decompofing water than the fulphuric
acid.

Other theorifts again tell us, that
the fulphuric acid unites firft to the
iron, and that the compound decompofes the water. But fhould not the
compound refulting from iron and fulphureous acid, as containing one half
lefs oxygen, produce the fame effect?
Even a man who is not a chemift-muft
fee the inconfiftency of fuch a doctrine.

It would be impoffible to detect the
fallacy of the above theory without the
aid of the experiment of the fulphureous acid, which fhews that abftracted
reafoning, be it ever fo plaufible, is
not to be relied upon.

The phœnomena of *day* and *night*
might appear equally well explained by
fuppofing the *fun* to revolve round the
earth, as the earth to turn round upon
its own axis, every twenty-four hours,

were

were our knowledge of aftronomy confined to thofe circumftances alone; but
it is by extending our views to the motion and harmony of the whole plane-
tary fyftem, that the delufion of fuch a
doctrine can only be detected. It is juft
fo with chemiftry; the concatenating a
few facts here and there, is not fufficient
to eftablifh a doctrine; it is neceffary
the theorift fhould traverfe the whole
field, accurately examine all the facts
upon record, find out their proper pofition and relation to each other, and
fee the arrangement, harmony, and
fymmetry of the whole fuperftructure
at one view; for that doctrine muft be
falfe which contradicts itfelf in any
one fingle point.

The theory of the decompofition of
water during the action of acids upon
the

the metals, is not the only inftance in
which I differ from the French chemifts; I only adduce it as being connected with the difcovery of the fulphureous acid, as a menftruum for
the analyfis of fteel.

Indeed, except that alone of the
nonentity of phlogifton, our mode of
reafoning is very different. They have
afferted the truth I will allow, but that
in an abftracted and unconnected manner, without fufficient conviction, for
all the phœnomena or facts adduced
feemed equally well explained upon
the phlogiftic principle.

I have connected the whole, and reduced it to a fyftem, and made ufe of
demonftrations, which in my opinion
are not to be invalidated or contra-
dicted, until the order of natural things
affume a different afpect.

Some

Some of my readers may probably suppose, before they enquire into this subject, that I exaggerate in my own behalf: But assumed modesty upon such an occasion as this, would be weakness indeed, and affected diffidence downright folly.

Every man who writes should deliberately weigh his opinions in the scale of his own understanding, and be convinced according to his judgment that he is right, before he presents them to the public. Every liberal minded man should also be open to conviction, and feel a pleasure in having his errors corrected: but until this happens, confidence and firmness are justifiable.

I will now conclude by observing, that one modification of the antiphlogistic doctrine escaped the French theorists rifts altogether; viz. the decompofition and recompofition of water during the oxygenation of metals, and I may add, other inflammable bodies, in the common temperature of the atmofphere.

This I have fhewn by experiment, with a view, principally, of proving the conftituent principles of water, which were difputed at the time. I fhall give the following fhort extract of it from my *Comparative View*, page 13. "Iron moiftened with water, and confined by mercury in a glafs cylinder, will yield inflammable air; iron, treated in the fame manner, and confined with dephlogifticated air, will produce no inflammable air, but the air will be diminifhed. Iron will yield no inflammable air if it be confined in very dry dephlogifticated air, neither will the

air

air be diminished, nor will the iron
tarnish, in *any* length of time; hence it
appears, that iron has no effect on air
in a common temperature, but that it
is the water which is decomposed, and
that the dephlogisticated air and the
inflammable air of the water unite at
the very instant of the liberation of
the latter, and recompose water.*"

From the foregoing data, it is evident that the decomposition of water
does not take place here, in conse-
quence of a double affinity occasioned
by the oxygen gas, as the iron alone
decomposes it, and liberates its hydrogen in a gasseous state.

That a metal should take oxygen
from hydrogen with more facility than
from

---

* When the above extract was published, the
new nomenclature was not adopted.

from caloric, which retains it with lefs
force, proceeds from two concurring
and oppofite caufes, viz. the aggregate
attraction of the ultimate particles of
the metal to each other on the one fide,
and on the other, partly from the affinity of oxygen to caloric, but principally from the diftance by which the
atmofpheres of caloric round each particle of oxygen keep them from the
furface of the metal, in a word, they
are by thefe means kept beyond the
ftriking diftance of their mutual attraction.   By way of analogy, I will
adduce a fingle fact to illuftrate this
point.—It is well known, that marine
acid has very ftrong affinity to calcareous earth, and yet perfectly pure
and dry calcareous earth will not condenfe dry marine acid gas, when both
are confined in a glafs cylinder over
mercury,

mercury, but as foon as a fmall quantity of water is introduced, the gas is
condenfed, and then unites to the calcareous earth.

Although water condenfes the marine acid gas, it has lefs affinity to it
by much than the calcareous earth, for
ftrictly fpeaking, water and marine
acid gas do not form a chemical
union. I am inclined to believe that
the affinity, or rather the capacity of
water for caloric, and its attraction to
the gravitating matter of the marine
gas at the fame time, although very
weak, co-operate with each other in
producing the effect. I alfo fufpect,
that a predifpofed affinity of water for
a portion of the caloric of the oxygen
gas, affifts the hydrogen, in its nafcent
ftate, to condenfe it fo as to conftitute
water,

d   The

The rapid and eafy condenfation of.
oxygen gas by nitrous gas, (which
have but a weak attraction to each
other) in the common temperature of
the atmofphere, takes place upon the
fame principle, and is a ftriking inftance of this kind of affinity proceed-
ing from caloric, for the compound
(*nitrous acid*) retains the whole of the
caloric of the oxygen gas in its condenfed ftate.   I am confident the
agency of caloric in this way, is
more general than chemifts are aware
of.

From the above ftatement, the circumftances which oppofe the union
of metals to oxygen gas are very obvious : But that metals, when the aggregate influence of their particles
upon each other, (being the principal
obftacle) is removed by caloric, are
capable

capable of decompofing oxygen gas,
and uniting directly to its bafe or gravitating matter, might be proved by a
variety of well connected facts, were
it confidered neceffary.

About four years ago, a very ingenious pamphlet appeared in the name of
a Mrs. Fulhame, in which this doctrine
of mine refpecting the decompofition
and recompofition of water has been
adduced and extended to every fpecies
of oxygenation, and even to the de-
oxydation of metals in every degree of
heat. I did not think myfelf warranted
when I had written, and much lefs fo
now, upon a more mature delibera-
tion, to apply it in that general way.

Had this fair author read my book,
and indeed I fuppofe fhe did not, (having quoted every other treatife upon
the

the fubject,) no doubt fhe would have been candid enough to do me the juftice of excepting *me* from the reft of my co-operators in fcience, when fhe told them they erred for having overlooked this modification of their doctrine, and alfo when fhe adduced it as an original idea of her own.

As to the reduction of metals, I have faid fo much already upon it, I have fcarcely any thing to add, for I have confidered the fubject in every poffible point of view, not excepting the agency of hydrogen in its nafcent ftate, when water is decompofed in contact with thofe oxyds which retain the oxygen with lefs force than hydrogen attracts it, as the following paragraph, taken from my *Comparative View*, page 280, will fhew.

" But

" But as water is prefent, a portion
" of it is alfo decompofed, by which
" means we obtain inflammable air.
" Whether the inflammable air itfelf
" at the inftant that it is deprived of
" its dephlogifticated air, may not con-
" tribute to the reduction of the mer-
" cury, by uniting to its dephlogifti-
" cated air, and reproducing water, is
" what I cannot pretend to determine;
" although from the attraction of the
" matter of light inflammable air to
" fire, together with the interference
" of the Pruffian acid, I am rather in-
" clined to fuppofe it does not."*

Although I do not agree with Mrs.
Fulhame, as to the decompofition of

water

---

* This relates to the reduction of the oxyd of
mercury, held in folution by the pruffic acid,
when iron filings and fulphuric acid are introduced.

water during the reduction of metals,
yet I confider her experiments very in-
terefting, and well worthy the attention
of chemical philofophers. It appears
from thofe ingenious experiments, that
the different metallic falts, that is, all
the metallic oxyds faturated with acids,
depofited into the interftices of filk in
a ftate of folution in water, were reduced by hydrogen gas in the ordinary
temperature of the atmófphere.

"The hydrogen of the gas," fays
fhe, "unites to the oxygen of the wa-
"ter, while the hydrogen of the latter
"unites in its nafcent ftate to the oxy-
"gen of the metal, reduces it, and
"forms water." She alfo fuppofes,
when charcoal is ufed, even in the
high temperatures, that water is decompofed, its oxygen uniting to the
carbon,

carbon, while its hydrogen unites to the oxygen of the metal and reduces it.

I would obferve, that the pure oxyds of metals, (thofe of the noble metals excepted) free from acids, or acid bafes, and depofited in filk, linen, or calico, and moiftened with water, will not be reduced by hydrogen in a common temperature, and fome of them not completely fo in any degree of heat; hence it follows, that the acid bafis it-felf acts a part here, which Mrs. Ful-hame was not aware of; befides, were hydrogen capable of reducing all the metals, its affinity to oxygen muft be fuperior to any of them, which a variety of well attefted facts will refute.

And again, if hydrogen were the re-ducer of all metallic oxyds, the differ-ent metals would not only precipitate

each

each other indifcriminately without
any order or marked affinity, from
their folution in acids, but *iron* would
precipitate *iron* in its metallic ftate;
copper would precipitate *copper*, and fo
with *tin* and *zinc* and all other metals.
It is, perhaps needlefs to enter more
largely into this fubject, therefore I
will drop it here.

I now beg leave to affure Mrs. F.
before we part, that I read her book
with great pleafure, and heartily wifh
her laudable example may be followed
by the reft of her fex; particularly by
thofe who poffefs talents and means
for making chemical experiments.

ESSAY

ESSAY

ON

BLEACHING.

SECTION I.

On Flax.

RIPE Flax when pulled out of the ground, is compofed of four diftinct fubftances, viz. a thin cortex, a green fap, the fibrous or flaxy part and the ligneous matter.

The fap or fucculent part is again compofed of an extractive matter and water, to feparate thefe different fub-ftances from the flaxy part, it muft firft be fubmitted to the following

B   procefs.

procefs. As foon as pulled it is to be
fteeped in foft water until the putre-
factive fermentation takes place.
This degree of fermentation com-
mences with the fucculent part as
being more fufceptible of decompofition than the reft, for the fermentation of animal or vegetable matter is a decompofition of their conftituent parts.

Were the flax to be continued long
in this ftate, the whole fubftance of it
would be decompofed or deftroyed
upon the fame principle that malt is
injured by too long fteeping, or that
wort lofes its fu bftance by too long a
fermentation It muft therefore be
taken out of the water while as yet
green, and before the whole of its fap
is feparated ; but by fpreading it thin
upon the ground, and expofing it to
the

the air, the remainder (being already on the wing of decompofition) is foon carried off or bleached out by the agency of the oxygenous part of the atmofphere.

Hard waters, which generally contain but a fmall portion of felenite (fulphat of lime) fometimes common falt and muriate of lime, injures the flax, for it foon rots when fteeped in fuch water. This circumftance feems difficult of folution.—We know very well that thefe faline fubftances are ftrong feptics in fmall quantities, but particularly the fulphat of lime which poffeffes this property in a higher degree than any other faline body, as obferved by Madame D. Arconville*
who,

* The wife of a prefident of Parliament at Bourdeaux.

who, it feems, has made a variety of experiments on the feptic powers of different faline fubftances.

I will alfo enumerate by way of analogy, the following ftriking facts, viz. that a fmall quantity of common falt will promote the putrefaction of flefh or fifh, while a larger quantity will preferve them—that a fmall quantity of falt taken with our aliment will promote digeftion, while an over dofe will produce the contrary effect—that a fmall portion of falt mixed with vegetable compofts, will help to fertilife, although a large quantity will render the foil fterile—and laftly, that fea water which contains falt but fparingly, will produce fimilar effect, with hard waters, upon

dead

dead animal and vegetable matter, but in ·a more eminent degree.

From thefe data onè is led to believe, that hard waters aɛ̃t too powerfully on the flax, by extending the putrefaɛ̃tive procefs or decompofttion to the fibrous, as well as the fucculent part, pretty much about the fame time. But to return, the flax when in a fit ftate to be taken off the ground, is of a greyifh white colour, very flexible and tenacious, and wholly free from the extraɛ̃tive matter or fap.

Nothing now remains but the wood and flax. The wood is an hollow little tube covered over very compaɛ̃tly with the flax; to feparate the wood it muft be kiln-dryed, in order to render it frangible or brittle, but care muft be taken not to apply too much heat for fear of injuring the flax. It is next to

be

be beat or broke, by which means the flax is not only divided into fmall fibres, but moft of the wood is feparated, and the part which adheres, is reduced to fmall fragments. To feparate thefe again, the flax is to be fcutched in fmall parcels at a time, either by manual labour or mills contrived for the purpofe.

Hackling is the laft procefs, which is nothing more than drawing, or if I may be allowed the expreffion, combing the flax in fmall parcels at a time, through a pile or group of polifhed and fharp iron fpikes placed firmly in wood thro' an iron plate. The fpikes are placed pretty clofe together; the firft hackle (for different hackles muft be ufed) is coarfe, the fecond finer, and the third finer again.

The

The procefs of hackling anfwers a double or triple purpofe; firft, it divides the fibres of the flax, as much as this can be effected by mechanical means; 2d, it feparates the minute fragments of wood which efcaped the procefs of fcutching; and laftly, it feparates the fhort coarfe flax, commonly called tow.

Spinning and weaving are too well known to need defcription, and alfo the preparation which the yarn requires previous to its being fet in the loom.

SECTION

SECTION II.

*On bleaching in the old method, with ge-
neral observations on the alkalies.*

THE linen as it comes from the
loom is charged with what is called the
weaver's dreffing, which is a pafte of
flour boiled in water, and as this is
brufhed into the yarn of the warp,
before it is wove, it is fomewhat difficult to feparate it when dry. To
difcharge this pafte, the linen muft be
fteeped in water for about forty eight
hours, when this extraneous fubftance
undergoes a kind of fermentation
which does not extend to the fubftance of the linen itfelf, upon the
fame principle that the green fap is
difengaged from the flax without in-
jury to its texture.

When

When the linen is well walhed after this laſt proceſs, it contains nothing that water can ſeparate; it is of a greyiſh white colour, although the fibres of which it is compoſed, when diveſted of every adventitious ſubſtance, are naturally very white.

The matter which thus colours the linen, is of a reſinous nature, inſoluble in water, and from its intimate union or diſſemination through the very fibres of the flax is difficult of ſeparation, even by thoſe ſubſtances which have a ſolvent power over it.

To diſengage it however, in as cheap and expeditious a manner as poſſible, without injuring the texture of the fabrick, is the ſole object of the proceſs of bleaching.

c   Pot-aſh

Pot-afh is the firft menftruum which fhould be ufed in bleaching; but perhaps it may not be amifs to make fome obfervations on its nature and general properties, before we apply it in this way.

All vegetable fubftances, from the fmalleft weed up to the oak, afford more or lefs afhes when burned in open air; which afhes contain different kinds of earths, neutral falts, and a fmall portion of pot-afh or alkali.

A given quantity of weeds yields more pot-afh than woods, as Mr. Kirwan has obferved in his excellent paper on alkalies, in the tranfactions of the Royal Irifh Academy for 1789.

I underftand the Irifh farmers burn their weeds (being in every other refpect ufelefs) every year, in order to obtain the alkali; hence it is needlefs to fay

any

any thing upon this head, only to observe, that pot-aſh is the ſame in whatever climate, or from whatever vegetable it is obtained.

The learned Dr. Watſon, formerly profeſſor of chemiſtry at the Univerſity of Cambridge, and now biſhop of Landaff, has ſhewn that 1300 tons of dry oak yield 15 tons of aſhes; and that theſe aſhes again afford only one ton of pot-aſh; hence it appears that we cannot expect any great ſupply in this country, but that we muſt ever look up to foreign nations, which abound with foreſts for this uſeful article.

To ſeparate the pot-aſh or alkali from the other ingredients in the aſhes, they muſt be put into ten or twelve times their weight of boiling water, or according to chemical language, *lixiviated*.

in

in water. By this means the pot-afh, (from its great folubility) together with the other faline fubftances, are diffolved, while the earthy part, being nearly infoluble, is left behind.

The folution or lixivium is to be drawn off clear from the dregs, and evaporated to drynefs in iron pots, and hence it is called pot-afh.

Pot-afh is far from being a pure falt; it contains from 20 to 25 per cent. of impurities, confifting principally of fulphat of pot-afh*and carbonic matter.

To free the pot-afh from carbon † or any other inflammable matter it may contain, it is expofed to the joint action

of

---

* Sulphat of pot-afh is a neutral falt, compofed of pure pot-afh and oil of vitriol, now called fulphuric acid.

† The term carbon is derived from carbo, the latin word for charcoal.

of air, and a moderate red heat, upon the bed of a reverberating furnace. Thus, the inflammable matter being burned out, the pot-afh, from being of a darkifh grey colour, acquires a pearly white; it is hence called pearl-afh.

Pearl-afh contains from 10 to 12 per cent. of impurities, moftly fulphat of pot-afh, and fometimes a fmall portion of muriate* of pot-afh. Thefe falts muft have been yielded by the wood, and diffolved by the large quantity of water neceffary to feparate the pot-afh from the afhes.

I more than once obtained near 20 per cent. of fulphat of pot-afh from the pearl-afh imported here; this great portion of fulphat of pot-afh could have never

---

* Muriate of pot-afh, a neutral falt, confifting of marine acid and pure pot-afh.

never been a natural product, but muſt have been an artificial adulteration ; and indeed, circumſtances have convinced me that it muſt be ſo.

During a mineralogical excurſion through England in the ſummer and autumn of the year 1785, the different manufactures which fell in my way, were not paſſed over. Upon enquiring of the diſtillers of aquafortis (nitrous acid) how they diſpoſed of the large reſiduum left in the ſtill (when the acid was carried over) which is ſulphat of pot-aſh, and which is of little or no uſe in the arts, they informed me it was bought up by the Iriſh merchants.

Sulphat of pot-aſh, when ground down, cannot readily be diſtinguiſhed as to its external appearance from pearl-aſh, and being ſo much cheaper than
the

the latter, is well calculated for the above fraudulent purpofe.

By no means do I intimate that this is a common practice, as from experience I know the contrary.

However, to pafs it over in filence would be unpardonable, when it is confidered that the bleacher is at the expence of an article of no ufe whatever in bleaching, and that, by the adulteration, the proportion beft known by experience to anfwer his purpofe is varied; by which means his procefs, although not altogether fruftrated, muft be materially retarded.

Sulphat of pot-afh is only foluble in about fixteen times its weight of water, in the temperature of 60°, while real pot-afh is foluble in its own weight of water, in the fame temperature; hence

hence they are eafily feparated in the
following fimple manner, viz. three
pounds of pearl-afh and two quarts of
water fhould boil together for a few
minutes, then be removed from the fire
and fuffered to ftand for twenty-four
hours, when the clear liquor is to be
decanted off. Half a pint more of cold
water is to be poured upon the dregs,
and this again drawn off when clear :
The infoluble falt is afterwards to be
well dried and weighed, which, being a
foreign falt, will give pretty nearly the
quantity of impurities in the pot-afh.

I would recommend the above mode
of analyfis to the bleachers before they
purchafe or ufe their pot-afh.

Common pot-afh when freed from
earthy, inflammable, and foreign faline
matter is ftill impure, being chemically

ly united to carbonic acid gas (fixable air*.) This combination does not altogether deprive it of its detergent property.

To obtain pot-afh perfectly pure, it muft be deprived of the carbonic acid: This is effected by quick lime, which has greater affinity to the acid than the pot-afh has.

The lime is to be flaked and fifted, and the pot-afh diffolved in water; then mixed and boiled†, and laftly, ftrained or filtered, or fuffered to fubfide. The clear liquor is a folution of pure pot-afh, and fhould not contain a particle of

D lime.

* Called carbonic acid, as the matter of charcoal is one of its conftituent principles.

† Upon a large fcale there is no neceffity for boiling the mixture, but to fuffer it to ftand for a few days before the pot-afh is drawn off. The mixture fhould be ftirred pretty often.

lime. This is what is commonly called soap-lye; the alkali requiring this treatment before it can make soap.

Pure pot-afh, according to our prefent knowledge of chemiftry, is a fimple elementary fubftance, and in this ftate, being uncombined or uninfluenced by any body whatfoever, its attraction is much encreafed for thofe fubftances to which it has affinity; fuch as fuet, oil, refins, gums, and in fhort, all animal and vegetable inflammable matter. Its attraction to animal matter is fuch, that it inftantly corrodes or diffolves the fkin and flefh of animals when brought into contact with them; hence it is called *cauftic lye* or *cauftic alkali*; while the carbonated pot-afh from being much weaker, is termed *mild alkali*.

It

It is upon the foregoing principle that foaps are made, which confift of animal or vegetable fats and pure alkaline lye. Soaps, although compofed of lye and oils, or greafe, or fats, are ftill poffeffed of a detergent property, that is to fay, they are capable of combining with more greafe or inflammable matter, and diffolving a large portion of it by the affiftance of heat. This comprehends the whole theory of wafhing or cleanfing of linen.

Mild pot-afh (the lye united to carbonic acid gas) is a more powerful detergent than foap; fo much fo, that its frequent ufe in the wafhing of linen would deftroy its texture, and wear it down too foon.

Cauftic lye or pure pot-afh has a fimilar effect with the mild, but in a higher

higher extreme; I would however fuppofe, that it might, when reduced, or fufficiently diluted with water, be advantageoufly fubftituted for foap in the cleanfing of coarfe linens, particularly in hofpitals.

Cauftic, or pure pot-afh, fhould ever be ufed by the bleachers, as having a greater folvent power over the colouring matter of the linen than the mild; befides, a given quantity of the former will go farther than the fame quantity of the latter.

The immediate application of lime to the linen, either by itfelf, or mixed with pot-afh, fhould be avoided; for although it has the property of bleaching, it deftroys the texture of the cloth. I have tried it in various ways and proportions, and don't hefitate to forbid the ufe of it.

The

The cauftic lye, it is true, unlefs properly diluted, is capable of injuring the cloth; and fo is fulphuric acid (oil of vitriol) which is known to be ufed with great fafety as a fouring.

Marine plants afford by incineration a fubftance poffeffing the fame property with pot-afh, particularly fo far as relates to bleaching and foap-making. This fubftance, being perhaps originally obtained from a marine plant called kali, hence derived the name alkali, which is now the common name for both fubftances; for hitherto, only two fixed alkalies, and one volatile have been difcovered, and perhaps in nature there are no more. The latter alkali is the product of the animal kingdom, and being remarkably volatile, is never ufed in bleaching.

The

The two fixed alkalies are diftinguifhed from each other by the names
vegetable alkali and *mineral alkali*, the
latter being found in great abundance
in the mineral kingdom, united to muriatic acid in the ftate of common falt.
It is found native, united only to carbonic acid gas, in hot climates, particularly in Egypt, and many other parts
of the Eaft, in a ftate of effloreſcence
upon the furface of the ground. It is
alfo found native in cold countries, particularly in Ruffia. Moft of what is
ufed in England and Ireland is extraŒt-
ed from the afhes of marine plants.
Thofe which come from Alicant, and
many countries bordering on the Me-
diterranean, are the richeſt. The plants
called foza, falicornia, gazulla, and
barilha, afford moft alkali; particu-

larly

larly the former and the latter; hence the afhes, which are a greyifh or bluifh black fufed mafs, go by the name of barilha; and the alkaline falt, when feparated from foreign impurities, is called foda.

The marine plants of our own fhores afford foda in very fmall proportions. Their afhes, which in external appearance cannot be readily diftinguifhed from barilha, are called kelp. The latter contains more foreign falts than the former, particularly fea falt. Thefe two fubftances are often mixed with each other, a fpecies of impofition not eafily detected but by analyfis. This is effected by boiling the afhes, firft reduced to powder, in thrice their weight of water, and then filtering the liquor. The refiduum on the filter is again to be boiled with half the quan-

tity

tity of water, and filtered or ftrained. The clear liquors are to be mixed while hot, and fet by to cryftallize.

Moft of the foda when extracted from either barilha or kelp, is cauftic, and will not cryftallize in that ftate; therefore the folution muft ftand five or fix days expofed to the air, in order to imbibe carbonic acid gas from the furrounding atmofphere, which contains more or lefs of this gas in every fituation. If the barilha be not good, it will not afford any cryftals in the above quantity of water; in this cafe it muft be evaporated down one-third, and fet by again*. When cryftallized, the mother-water

---

* I frequently failed in the cryftallization of foda in every degree of ftrength in the liquor, until evaporated down to perfect drynefs, and redifolved again in frefh water, when it readily cryftallized; but whenever this happened, the barilha was not of the beft kind.

water is to be decanted off, and evaporated down one half; during this
fecond evaporation, if it contain much
fea-falt, that falt will make its appearance, and cryftallize in the hot liquor;
being no more foluble in hot water
than in cold; this is feparated by
ftraining the folution while hot.

The liquor on cooling will depofit
a fecond crop of cryftals of foda, at the
fame time that the common falt will
remain in folution. This procefs muft
be repeated, every fubfequent mother
liquor being partly evaporated, until as
much as poffible of the foda is obtained*.

This kind of treatment is fufficient
for the bleacher's purpofe, the quantity
of alkali being his only object. For a

E   more

---

* Good barilha contains from fifteen to fixteen
per cent. of cryftallized foda more than kelp.

more accurate analyfis of the different materials contained in the barilha, fee Kirwan on alkaline fubftances. *Irifh tranfaƈtions for* 1789.

The bleachers, when they ufe foda, avoid the expence and trouble of extraƈting it from the afhes; they charge the barilha in powder into a coarfe linen bag, and boil it with the cloth, thus the alkaline part is extraƈted by the water, while the infoluble dregs remain behind in the bag, which fhould be of thick canvas, and being already pretty nearly in a cauftic ftate, the mediation of quick-lime is unneceffary.

From the foregoing outlines of the general properties of alkalies, particularly thofe of pot-afh, which is the alkali moft frequently ufed, it is eafy to conceive what part it aƈts in the bleaching of linen.

The

The pot-afh or alkali, from its folvent power over the colouring matter,
diffolves and feparates the part imme-
diately expofed to its action; that is to
fay, the part of it which refts fuperficially upon the fibres of the flax or
thread; I fay fuperficially, for it requires
ten or twelve repeated boilings at
leaft, with the alternate agency of the
atmofphere, to feparate the whole of
the refin.

It might be afked, why fuch an ac-
tive folvent as pot-afh fhould not carry
away the entire of the refin at once, or
at leaft as much as it *alone* could in
any way feparate.—This requires an
explanation.

What appears to us to be a fingle
ultimate fibre of flax in grey linen, is
com, ofed of a bundle of minute filaments, clofely cemented or agglutinat-
ed

ed together by the refinous matter; therefore the pot-afh firft ufed only acts upon the refin of the external coating of filaments, by which means they are loofened or feparated, and expofed to the further action of the air.

The fecond boiling in pot-afh opens a fecond layer, and thus fucceffively layer after layer until the entire is divided or opened to the centre.

Were the folution of pot-afh fufficiently ftrong to force its way at once to the centre, it would act upon the filaments themfelves and deftroy the texture of the cloth.

Each filament, after the procefs of pot-afh, retains an impregnation of colouring matter, fo intimately united as to refift the further action of it. This can only be removed by the flow and gradual influence of the atmofphere.

But

But upon what principle does at-
mofpheric air act? To underftand this
clearly, a previous knowledge of the
nature and properties of it, is abfolutely
neceffary.

The atmofphere in which we are
immerfed, and which furrounds this
globe we inhabit, preffes upon every
fquare inch of its furface with about
the weight of fourteen pounds. It is
compofed of two fluids or airs, me-
chanically mixed or diffufed through
each other (to compare denfer bodies
to rarer) like fpirits and water, or fu-
gar and water. One hundred parts of
this air contain only twenty-feven, capable of fupporting combuftion or animal life; hence called vital air; the
other feventy-three parts are the re-
verfe of it in both thefe refpects, and
are

are called azotic gas*. By burning a body in the air, or by the refpiration of animals, the vital part (now called oxygen gas†) is abforbed and feparated from the azotic gas which is left behind, and which extinguifhes bodies in combuftion, and kills animals. Thus by combuftion and refpiration, an analyfis of the atmofphere is effected.

Moft inflammable bodies refift the attraction of the oxygenous part of the atmofphere in a common, or even in a much higher temperature. This proceeds

---

* Azot is derived from the Greek privative, particle *a* and ξωή, *vita* from its quality of killing animals in the act of breathing it.

† Called oxygen gas, as being one of the conftituent principles of all acids, and it is fuppofed that an acid cannot exift without its prefence. It is derived from the Greek οξυς, *acidum*, and γεινομαι, *gignor*. Hence a compound word fignifying the acid-getting principle.

ceeds from two caufes, which co-operate with each other: The one, from the attraction of caloric * (the matter of heat) to the gravitating or folid matter of oxygen gas. The other proceeds from the attraction of aggregation, or that influence which the moft minute or ultimate particles of all folid bodies exert upon each other in a higher or lefs degree.

Thus, for example, Carbon or fulphur, although both highly inflammable, will not burn in contact with air, until this influence is in a great meafure done away: This is effected by an high temperature, or in other words, by caloric, which penetrates between their particles. By this means they are removed beyond each others

---

* Caloric, the matter of heat, derived from *alor* the latin for heat.

others mutual influence, and confequently are left at liberty to direct the
whole of their attraction towards the
oxygenous part of the atmofphere.

The fire or caloric evolved during
the act of combuftion, comes from the
air ; the burning body, from fuperior affinity to its oxygen, only liber-
ating the caloric from its chemical union
with it : for caloric chemically united,
is not felt, nor does it act as caloric ;—
juft as cryftallized falts which contain
half their weight of water, will not
wet or feel moift to the hand, or as
fulphuric or nitrous acid, when united
to an alkali, will not corrode.

From the above ftatement of the
properties of oxygen gas and pot-afh,
their *modus operandi* is very obvious.
The pot-afh diffolves in each boiling,
a certain

a certain quantity of the colouring matter, and partly divides the filaments of each fibre of the flax; the oxygen gas, in its turn, unites to the portion ftill adhering to thofe filaments that eluded the action of potafh, with which it forms carbonic acid gas*. The carbonic acid gas, from its volatility, flies off and mixes with the atmofphere.

Thus alternately, the one diffolving and the other burning out (for bleaching is flow combuftion) the linen is whitened.

* Water is alfo formed in proportion to the quantity of hydrogen the refin contains.

F   SECTION

SECTION III.

*On bleaching with the oxygenated muriatic
acid, and on the methods of preparing it.*

As atmofphcric air is the moft tardy
menftruum in bleaching, requiring as
many days and nights upon the green,
as hours in pot-afh, it has ever been
confidered a great object to accelerate
its combination with the colouring
matter.

To promote the fpeedy action of at-
mofpheric air, or rather the oxygenous
part of it, in its ordinary elaftic ftate,
is well known to be impoffible.

The prefent advanced ftate of chemiftry, however, has enabled us indirectly

to

to obviate thofe obftacles. Firft, by condenfing or combining the oxygen of the atmofphere, with fubftances to which it has great affinity; 2dly, by transferring it again from thofe fubftances, to others to which it has lefs affinity, but fufficient attraction to retain it in a concentrated ftate; and laftly, by fteeping the linen in this laft compound, which readily imparts its oxygen to the colouring matter.

In order to be more explicit, I will obferve, that moft metallic bodies have ftrong attraction to oxygen gas; for inftance, lead when melted, or penetrated by a fufficiency of the matter of heat, fo as to remove its aggregate influence, will drink in, if I may be allowed the expreffion, one twelfth of its own weight of oxygen.

Py

By this union, the lead lofes its metallic brilliancy and cohefion, and af-
fumes a loofe earthy appearance and
reddifh colour, hence called *red-lead*.

When fulphuric acid (*oil of vitriol*)
is poured upon red-lead, part of its
oxygen is expelled in an aëriform ftate,
that is, combined with caloric.

All metals thus united to oxygen,
are called oxyds, diftinguifhed from
each other by the name of their refpective metals; as for inftance, oxyd
of lead, of iron, of tin, of copper, &c.

Hence it appears, that metals, being
in themfelves fixed bodies, are the
fitteft fubftances to withdraw oxygen
gas from the atmofphere, and to fix
and concentrate it.

Some metals, but particularly a
black femi-metallic fubftance called
manganefe,

manganefe, are found in the ftate of oxyds in the bowels of the earth. Manganefe, from its great affinity to oxygen, is never found in any other ftate.

Manganefe, as well as the reft of the oxyds, will not impart its oxygen to the colouring matter of the linen even in a boiling heat, when diffufed in water, or in any temperature fhort of that which would deftroy the texture of the cloth.

The oxygen therefore, thus collected, and attached to the metal muft, as obferved above, be transferred to another fubftance which retains it with lefs force, and confequently imparts it more freely to the furface of the linen. To effect this, the following are the materials and proportion ufed, viz. the oxyd of manganefe fixty pounds, common

mon falt fixty pounds, and fulphuric acid fifty pounds* diluted with its own bulk of water†.

The manganefe is to be finely ground and well mixed with the falt, and charged into a leaden ftill, fufficiently capacious to hold forty gallons of water, in order to allow fpace for the fwelling of the ingredients during their chemical action upon each other, which, at the commencement of the procefs, is very confiderable.

The ftill fhould be rather of a conical form, that is, fomewhat progreffively widening from the bottom to nearly

---

* Called fulphuric acid, fulphur being the bafis, and oxygen the other principle.

† Forty-five pounds of good fulphuric acid, of fuch fpecific gravity that a pint will weigh twenty-nine ounces, will be found fuffi‑ cient, when inftead of plain water, the acidulous liquor in the middle receiver is added, which will hereafter be defcribed.

nearly the upper part. The mouth or aperture of this apparatus is to be fitted with a flat or conical leaden cover, which is to reft in a groove, and the junctures are to be luted with well tempered blue clay.

An iron rod or upright, covered over with lead, is to be fixed in the centre of the cover as tight as poffible, without impeding a rotatory motion.— It fhould reach to the bottom of the ftill with prongs or wings to that part which enters the charge, in order, occafionally, to mix the materials, and to bring all their parts to act upon each other.

A leaden funnel fhould alfo be inferted, air tight, into another part of the cover, with a long ftem which fhould curve upright a few inches underneath it. This will prevent the
escape

efcape of the elaftic fluids, difengaged,
during the charging of the fulphuric
acid upon the materials, which would
be highly injurious to the workmen.

It is, I fhould fuppofe, unneceffary
to explain the principle upon which
the curved funnel acts, fuffice it then
to fay, that two columns of fulphuric acid of equal weight, the one in
the curved part, and the other in the
perpendicular, reft in the ftem of the
funnel, which balance each other, and
which, by their gravity, prefs againft
the expanfive force of the internal elaftic fluid.—Were the ftem of the funnel ftraight, the elaftic fluids would
fometimes make their efcape, even
againft the current of the fulphuric
acid paffing through it.

A leaden

A leaden tube, three inches diameter in the bore, and of convenient length, fhould communicate from the cover to a leaden receiver large enough to hold about eight gallons.

This is to contain water only, and fhould betwo-thirds filled with it; another tube of the fame diameter with the former fhould pafs from this receiver, above the level of the water, to the upper part of a veffel, or cafk fufficiently capacious to hold eight hundred gallons of water, and eighty pounds of well-flated and fifted quick-lime.

As the lime, from its fuperior fpecific gravity to water, would fink in it and fall to the bottom of the receiver, it is neceffary to ufe fome means of keeping it fufpended. For this purpofe, an upright agitator, fuch as was recommend-

G   ed

ed for the leaden ftill, fhould be adopted here; but the latter is to be of wood. By this contrivance a rotatory motion may be communicated to the liquor at pleafure. Two or three boards or wings fhould alfo be fixed to the fides of the cafk at right angles; the liquor, by dafhing againft thofe, will acquire additional motion. Thus a continual furface of frefh lime liquor will be prefented during the procefs, to the oxygenated muriatic acid gas, which will much facilitate its condenfation.

This fhort defcription will give a fufficient idea of the apparatus, and of the expence attending it. Thofe who ufe it, I underftand, find it very convenient, but doubtlefs practice will improve it. The apparatus itfelf may be feen at work at the bleach-green of

Charles

Charles Duffin, at Dungannon*. A
.Mr. Tennant who works for him, and
who, it feems, is very expert at the
procefs, may be employed by the different bleachers, until they get into the
method of managing it themfelves.

As the lead would be liable to melt,
if expofed to a naked fire, in confe-
quenceof the folid materials refting upon the bottom of it, and as the heat
of boiling water- is fufficient to work
the charge, the ftill fhould be placed in
a copper or iron boiler, large enough to
admit a fufficient quantity of water to
furround it.

The apparatus being thus difpofed,
it remains now to attend to the theory
and management of the procefs.

The

---

* Since the above was written, I have been
informed, that no lefs than thirty fuch apparatus
are now ufed in the north of Ireland.

The oxyd of the manganefe and falt being charged into the ftill, the cover luted on, and the whole of the apparatus being connected together, the fulphuric acid is to be gradually poured on by means of the curved funnel. The fulphuric acid, the inftant it comes in contact with the other materials, acts partly upon the falt, while another portion of it unites to the manganefe.

Manganefe is an oxyd, a metal faturated with oxygen gas: Common falt is compofed of muriatic acid gas and an alkaline falt called foda, the fame which barilha affords: Manganefe has a greater affinity to fulphuric acid than it has to the oxygen*, and the foda of the falt greater affinity to fulphuric acid than to the muriatic acid gas; hence it neceffarily

---

* The quantity of oxygen neceffary to metallic folution is excepted here.

ceffarily follows, that thefe two gafes,
(or rather their gravitating matter,) muft
be liberated from their former union in
immediate contact with each other;
and, although they have but a weak
affinity to one another, they unite in
their nafcent ftate, that is to fay, before
they individually unite to caloric, and
feparately affume the gaffeous ftate;
for oxygen gas, and muriatic acid gas,
already formed, will not unite when
mixed, in confequence principally of
the diftance at which their refpective
atmofpheres of caloric keep their gravitating particles afunder*.

The

* Common muriatic acid, that is, water faturated with muriatic acid gas, poured upon the
manganefe, will afford the oxygenated muriatic
gas; but as the acid muft firft be difengaged from
the falt, by means of fulphuric acid, and diftilled,
this would be an expenfive method.

The compound refulting from thefe two gafes, ftill retains the property of affuming the gaffeous ftate, and is the oxygenated muriatic gas.

Heat fhould not be applied until the firft action of the fulphuric acid upon the dry materials, (which is rather confiderable) nearly fubfides, otherwife the oxygenated muriatic gas will be generated fafter than it can be condenfed, which would endanger a rupture of the veffels.

At the commencement of the procefs, a portion of the muriatic acid gas efcapes uncombined with oxygen gas, which were it condenfed in the oxygenated liquor, would be rather injurious to it; but common muriatic gas, being more condenfable in water than the oxymuriatic gas, is arrefted and condenfed in the middle or leaden receiver; —fuch is the principal ufe of this part

of

of the apparatus. The pure oxygen gas paffes into the wooden receiver, where it is abforbed by the lime, and the compound, being a foluble fubftance, is diflolved by the water in the condenfer.

This liquor is the oxygenated muriate of lime, and may, foon after the procefs is over, be drawn off clear from the infoluble dregs, which in a fhort time fubfide to the bottom. In this ftate, it is of fufficient ftrength to bear thrice its bulk of water for the purpofe of bleaching. .

The refiduum in the ftill confifts of fulphat of manganefe, fulphat of foda, a fmall portion of muriate of manganefe, and fome oxyd of manganefe which efcaped the action of the acids. The latter fubftance being infoluble, the different falts may be feparated from it by by means of hot water. This refiduary manganefe, when well wafhed and dryed, may be ufed over again in a frefh charge.

The oxygenated muriatic acid gas was firft difcovered by the immortal SCHEELE, a celebrated Swedifh chemift.

The application of it in the art of bleaching, was referved for BERTHOL- LET, a famous French chemift, who firft recommended it condenfed in plain water. This method, however well it may anfwer in fmall experiments, was afterwards found inconvenient in the large way; for firft, the water condenfes the gas fo very fparingly, that the apparatus ufed muft neceffarily be upon too large and expenfive a fcale. 2dly, Water condenfes the gas fo flowly, the procefs muft be tedious, for the charge cannot be worked fafter than the gas is abforbed;

ed; and laftly, water retains the gas fo very weakly, that it is continually flying off during the application of the liquor, and is not only loft, but highly injurious to the workmen.

Hence this method had been afterwards fuperfeded by a folution of pure pot-afh, which was found to obviate the above inconveniencies, by more effectually condenfing and fixing the gas.

Although the oxygenated muriate of pot-afh has been ufed with great advantage by the paper-makers, it does not appear to have made any great progrefs in our bleach-greens.

What fuccefs the oxygenated muriate of lime may be attended with, I will not at prefent take upon me to fay; this can only be afcertained by the progrefs it will make amongft the moft

enlightened

enlightened of the bleachers, who are ever ready to adopt every means likely to fave labour and expence. I muft, however, obferve, from a feries of comparative experiments which I made upon it and the oxygenated pot-afh, by order of the Linen Board, that the former, as being cheaper, and lefs liable to injure the texture of the cloth, has decidedly the preference.

By the experiments I made, it appeared, that fix boilings in pot-afh and alternate fteepings in the oxygenated lime-liquor, bleached the linen well; but it was liable to turn yellowifh by boiling in foap, or repeated wafhings: Hence it was found neceffary to bleach the linen partly in the common way firft.

According

According to the information I have received from Mr. Duffin, the following is the method practised by those bleachers who use the oxymuriate of lime, viz. 1st, four boilings in pot-ash, and four weeks expofure to the air, 2dly, two immerfions in the oxygenated lime, with an alternate boil in pot-ash, and a week's grafs between each boiling or immerfion; after this treatment the linen is fit for the boards and fours.

During the fummer months two boilings in pot-ash, and a fortnight's expofure to the air is fufficient to prepare the linen for the oxygenated liquor; after this, three boilings in the alkali, and alternate fteeps in the oxygenated muriate of lime will finish it.

From

From the foregoing view of the theory and practice of bleaching, it is evident, that whether the linen be bleached in the ufual way by the tardy procefs of expofing the cloth to the action of the oxygen gas of the atmof-phere, or by the more expeditious method of ufing the oxygenated liquor as an auxiliary, the ufe of pot-afh, or a *fubftitute* for it, is indifpen-fably neceffary. How far I have been fuccefsful as to fuch a fubftitute, the following fection will evince.

SECTION

SECTION IV.

On sulphuret of lime, as a substitute for pot-ash.

SINCE I had the honour of being appointed chemist to the Linen Board, which is now more than three years, I have allotted a confiderable portion of my time and attention to the inveftigation of the principles of that fcience, applicable to the art in which I am thus more particularly interefted. It appeared, that until pot-afh could be difpenfed with, we muft for ever remain in the power of foreign nations as to our ftaple commodity: Obferving alfo, that all the late improvements in bleaching were exclufively confined to the one object—that of imparting

parting oxygen to the cloth, in a fafe and expeditious manner, but that there had been no effort made to fuperfede the neceffity of pot-afh, by far the moft expenfive and uncertain article employed by the bleacher, and for which he is entirely dependent upon foreign markets; I directed my attention chiefly to difcover a fubftitute for pot-afh; which, provided it fhould be of Irifh production, though it might be equally expenfive, I conceived would be of the utmoft national importance. Imprefled with thefe ideas, I undertook a feries of experiments with that view.

To enumerate the many difappointments and failures I experienced during my inveftigation, would be endlefs, and an unneceffary intrufion

upon

upon my reader.—Knowing, from an important obfervation of Mr. Kirwan, that faline hepars, or the combination of an alkali with fulphur, might, from its detergent properties be advantageoufly employed in bleaching, as a fubftitute for mere alkali, by an obvious analogy I was led to expect a fimilar effect from calcareous hepar, or, more properly fpeaking, fulphuret of lime, being a combination of lime and fulphur.

In thefe expectations I was not difappointed, but at that time (about three years fince) I contented myfelf (rather through neceffity, for large cities are very unfavourable to experiments on bleaching by expofure to the atmofphere,) with pointing it out to fome of the principal bleachers from the north then in town, earneftly recommending

commending it to them to give it a
fair trial with; and without pot-afh.
Since that time, alkaline falts having
become progreffively dearer, and in
confequence of a late propofal of fub-
ftituting lime for pot-afh, in condenfing the oxymuriated gas, I was
inftigated to refume the fubject, and
make further and more varied trials.
The refult of which has been, that the
ufe of the fulphuret of lime may be moft
advantageoufly combined with that of
the oxymuriated lime, and that thus
cloth may be perfectly whitened without the ufe of a particle of alkali.
This then alone would feem to give it
a decided preference over the methods
at prefent in ufe, while at the fame
time it poffeffes peculiar advantages,
and is exempt from the principal ob-
jections to which other *fubftitutes* are
liable;

liable; for 1ft quicklime and fulphur, the materials of which the *calcareous hepar* confifts, are both articles of trivial expence, efpecially as the latter enters but fparingly into the compofition; 2dly, their combination is effected in the eafieft and moft expeditious manner poffible, and perfectly level with the capacity of the meaneft workman; 3dly, as the manner of its application is, by fteeping the cloth in it cold, the faving of fuel is a matter of great magnitude; and laftly, there is no danger to be apprehended in the ufe of it, from the unfkilfulnefs or negligence of the workman, as it appears to be incapable of injuring the texture of the cloth.

The *fulphuret* of *lime* is prepared in the manner following:—Sulphur, or brimftone in fine powder, four pounds, lime well flaked and fifted twenty

I pounds;

pounds, water fixteen gallons ; thefe
are all to be well mixed and boiled for
about half an hour in an iron veffel,
ftirring them brifkly from time to
time. Soon after the agitation of
boiling is over, the folution of the fulphuret of lime clears, and may be
drawn off free from the infoluble
matter, which is confiderable, and
which refts upon the bottom of the
boiler*. The liquor in this ftate, is
pretty nearly of the colour of fmall
beer, but not quite fo tranfparent.

Sixteen gallons of frefh water are afterwards to be poured upon the infoluble
dregs in the boiler, in order to feparate
the whole of the fulphuret from them.

When

* Although *lime* is one of the conftituent principles of the *fulphuret*, yet being fo intimately
united to the fulphur, it has no longer the property of lime ; upon the fame principle that
fulphuric acid in fulphat of pot-afh, has not the
property of that acid.

When this clears (being previoufly well agitated) it is alfo to be drawn off and mixed with the firft liquor ; to thefe again, thirty three gallons more of water may be added, which will reduce the liquor to a proper ftandard for fteeping the cloth.

. Here we have, (an allowance being made for evaporation, and for the quantity retained in the dregs) fixty gallons of liquor from four pounds of brimftone.

Although fulphur by itfelf is not in any fenfible degree foluble in water, and lime but very fparingly fo, water diffolving but about one feven-hundredth part of its weight of lime ; yet the fulphuret of lime is highly foluble*.

* When the above proportion of lime and fulphur is boiled with only twelve gallons of water, the fulphuret partly cryftallizes upon cooling, and when once cryftallized, it is not eafy of folution. .

SECTION

SECTION V.

On bleaching with the sulphuret of lime.

WHEN the linen is freed from the weaver's dressing, in the manner already described, it is to be steeped in the solution of sulphuret of lime (prepared as above) for about twelve or eighteen hours, then taken out and very well washed ; when dry, it is to be steeped in the oxymuriate of lime for twelve or fourteen hours, and then washed and dried. This process is to be repeated six times, that is, six alternate immer-

immerſions in each liquor, which I found ſufficient to whiten the linen.

When I ſubmitted the linen to ſix boilings in pot-aſh, and to ſix immer- ſions in the oxygenated liquor, is was not better bleached than the above.

The three firſt boilings in pot-aſh, it is true, produced a ſomewhat better effeƐt than as many ſteeps' in the ſul- phuret ; but towards the concluſion, that is, when the linen was bleached, the ſmalleſt difference was not obſerv- able as to colour. The linen bleached with the pot-aſh was thinner, or more impoveriſhed than that treated with ſulphuret, and the latter ſtood the teſt of boiling with ſoap much better than the former, although it did acquire a ſlight yellowiſh tinge, which I ſhould ſuppoſe a week's, or at moſt, a fort- night's graſs, as they term it, would re- move.

I con-

I contrafted the effects of hot and
cold fulphuret in various temperatures,
and although ·the difference appeared
in favour of the hot liquor, yet it was
fo trifling as not to deferve confideration, or the expenditure of the fmalleft
quantity of fuel.

When I fteeped the linen in the fulphuret firft, and afterwards boiled it
in pot-afh, and then immerfed it once
in the oxygenated liquor, a better effect was produced, than from two
previous boilings in pot-afh, or from
two ·fteeps in the fulphuret; fo that
the two fubftances feem to co-operate
with each other.

Indeed, from what I have feen, two
fucceffive fteeps in frefh fulphuret, previous to the immerfion in the oxygenated liquor, feemed to afford very little

tle better effect than a single one, which is not the cafe with refpect to pot-afh.

It was obfervable, that the cloth was invariably thicker or more fwelled coming out of the fulphuret, than after being boiled in pot-afh, and remained fo when even wafhed and dried.

It appears to me, that the fulphuret opens the fibres of the linen more fpeedily and better than the latter, by foftening and fwelling, rather than by diffolving, the refinous or colouring matter. This accounts for the better effect of pot-afh upon the linen when previoufly fteeped in the fulphuret, than when ufed by itfelf.

Probably thofe bleachers who do not at prefent find it convenient to ufe the oxygenated liquor, but continue to bleach by expofure to air, may derive

fome

fome advantage from this, by ufing the fulphuret and pot-afh conjointly or alternately.

Mr. John Duffy, of Ball's-bridge, (who from his knowledge of chemif- try is very well acquainted with the principles of bleaching) was kind enough to repeat the above experi- ments, and his report to me corref- ponded with my own obfervations.

It is almoft impoffible to afcertain to the full extent, more efpecially by fmall experiments in an elaboratory, the many advantages any fubftance not hitherto ufed in bleaching, will af- ford by varying the mode of applica- tion.

The experimenter does a great deal by difcovering the efficacy, proving the practicability, and afcertaining the fafeft and moft economical method of

directly

directly ufing it, and alfo the beft proportion of it. Before he can ar- rive at any one of thefe, many a round of changes are neceffary; indeed a greater number than any man who is not ufed to experiments can be aware of. But I fhould hope, that the bleacher need not hefitate to ufe it in the ftate in which I prefent it to him, more efpecially as he runs no rifque of injuring the cloth with it. If he can make more of it hereafter, I fhall feel happy upon the occafion; no dif- covery was ever brought to perfection at once.

How gradually, and yet how pro- greffively the fteam engine, from its firft invention by the Marquis of Worcefter, was brought to its prefent degree of perfection? Undoubtedly, it was juft fo with refpect to alkalies,

K   the

the fubftances now ufed by the bleachers, it muft have taken a confiderable
time after their firft application in
bleaching, before they could be made
the moft of.

I will now conclude by pointing out
the advantage likely to accrue from
the ufe of the fulphuret, to the nation, and alfo the faving to the individual.

By the information I have had
from the Cuftom Houfe, it appears
that the average importation of pot-
afh, pearl-afh and barilha, the laft
twelve years, amounts to about 5066
tons annually ; about one half of this,
(2533 tons) is barilha. The average
price of barilha the laft three years,
has been forty pounds a ton, fo that
the value of the quantity imported is
101,323

101,323 pounds; of this only half, or thereabout, I underſtand, is uſed in bleaching, the remainder being converted into ſoap.

Moſt of the pot and pearl-aſh is conſumed by the bleachers, and the average price of it the laſt three years has been ſixty-five pounds a ton, conſequently, the value of 2,533 tons is 164,645 pounds.

Hence it ſeems, that the quantity of foreign alkalies imported into the kingdom every year, amounts to 265,968 pounds; and that the quantity uſed in bleaching alone, amounts to about 215,307 pounds annually.

The average price of brimſtone for the laſt three years, is about twenty-five pounds a ton, which is at the rate nearly of two pence farthing a pound;

pound; four pounds of brimftone, and twenty pounds of lime, as already obferved, will produce fixty gallons of liquor.   In this country, twenty pounds of lime may be valued at about four pence, fo that the bleacher may have the fixty gallons at the expence of 1s. 1d.

By what I could learn from different bleachers, the common allowance of alkali for fixty gallons of water, is fix pounds of barilha or four pounds of pot-afh at the very leaft, and moft bleachers ufe more than this. The price of four pounds of pot-afh at the rate of fixty five pounds a ton, is about two fhillings and four pence, which is two pence more than double the price of the fulphuret; but as the brimftone muft be ground, an allow-

ance

ance fhould be made for it ;   and being eafy of pulverization, a farthing
per pound is an ample confideration
for the expence attending it.

The faving of fuel only remains
now to be taken into confideration;
and as this cannot be calculated with
any degree of accuracy, I fhall con-
tent myfelf by particularizing facts.
In the firft place, but fixteen gallons
of liquid are to be boiled in preparing
fixty gallons of the fulphuret, while
the whole fixty gallons muft be boiled
when the alkali is ufed; hence it
might appear that two thirds of the
fuel are faved in the quantity of liquor,
but it is not quite fo much, fuppofe
we eftimate it at one half, which is
rather under-rating it.   Let us add
to this the time neceffary to boil the
different

different liquors; the fulphuret requires but about half an hour, and
the alkaline lixivium at the very leaft,
feven hours to boil the linen in it,
which is in the proportion of one to
fourteen.

The faving altogether to the bleacher
from this ftatement, is obvioufly very
confiderable; and as the Wicklow
copper mines are fufficient to fupply
the whole kingdom, or indeed two
fuch kingdoms with abundance of
fulphur, let the confumption be ever
fo great, the entire of the alkali, or
215,307 pounds muft be annually
faved to the nation.

But fuppofe two thirds only of the
quantity of alkali generally con-
fumed in bleaching were difpenfed
with

with by the ufe of the fulphuret (which is a fuppofition not warranted by my experiments) 'ftill the faving to the nation and to the individual, muft evidently be great indeed.

THE END.

www.ingramcontent.com/pod-product-compliance
Lightning Source LLC
Chambersburg PA
CBHW031443280326
41927CB00038B/1577